THE VERY BIG VERY RIGGED ELECTION

C.G. ROUSING

ISBN: 978-1-7340594-4-1

FOR FOREST

PATRIOTS EVERYWHERE

AND FREEDOM

THE VERY BIG VERY RIGGED ELECTION

RED-PILL A FRIEND TODAY.

IT'S THE AMERICAN WAY.

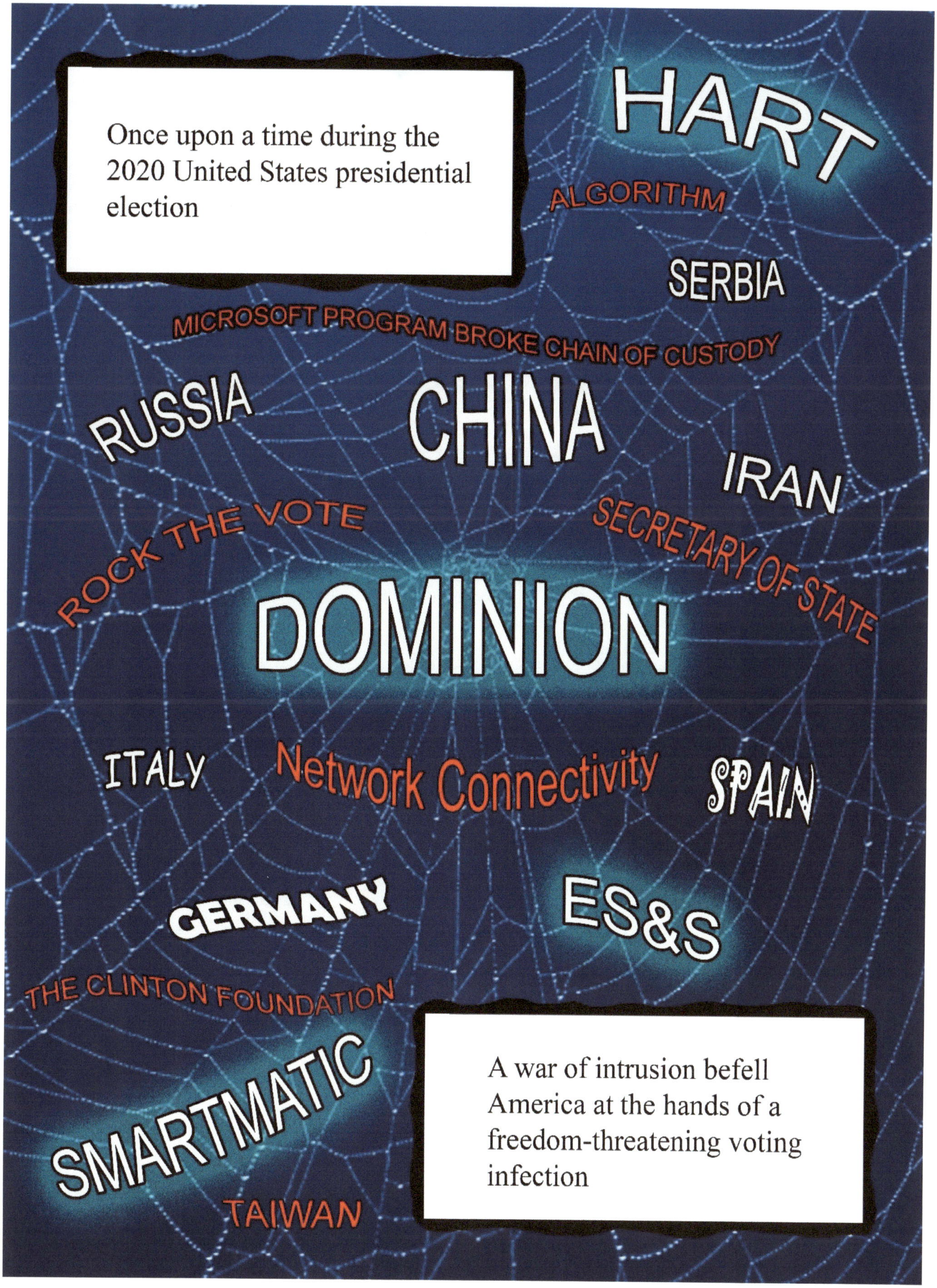

Once upon a time during the 2020 United States presidential election

HART

ALGORITHM

SERBIA

MICROSOFT PROGRAM BROKE CHAIN OF CUSTODY

RUSSIA

CHINA

IRAN

ROCK THE VOTE

SECRETARY OF STATE

DOMINION

ITALY

Network Connectivity

SPAIN

GERMANY

ES&S

THE CLINTON FOUNDATION

SMARTMATIC

TAIWAN

A war of intrusion befell America at the hands of a freedom-threatening voting infection

Stealthy software
By Smartmatic
With technology
Licensed by Dominion

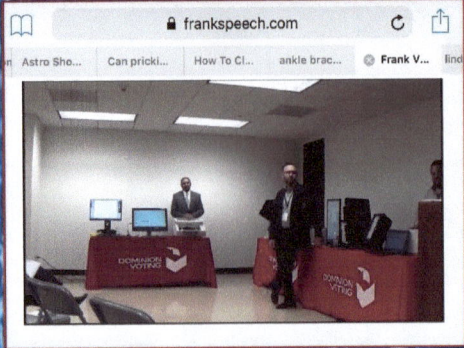

#FrankSpeech

Absolute Proof

100% CYBER ATTACK

#MyPillow

Absolute Interference

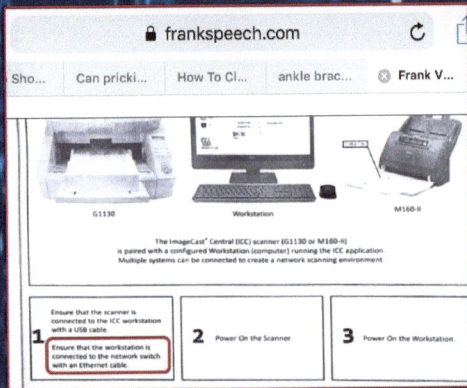

Deleted mega votes for Trump
Some say in the millions

A winner was to be determined
By 8:00 pm
On the 3rd of November

When Trump was
winning by a landslide
And liberals would soon
be forced to surrender

But oddly many states simply ceased their counting

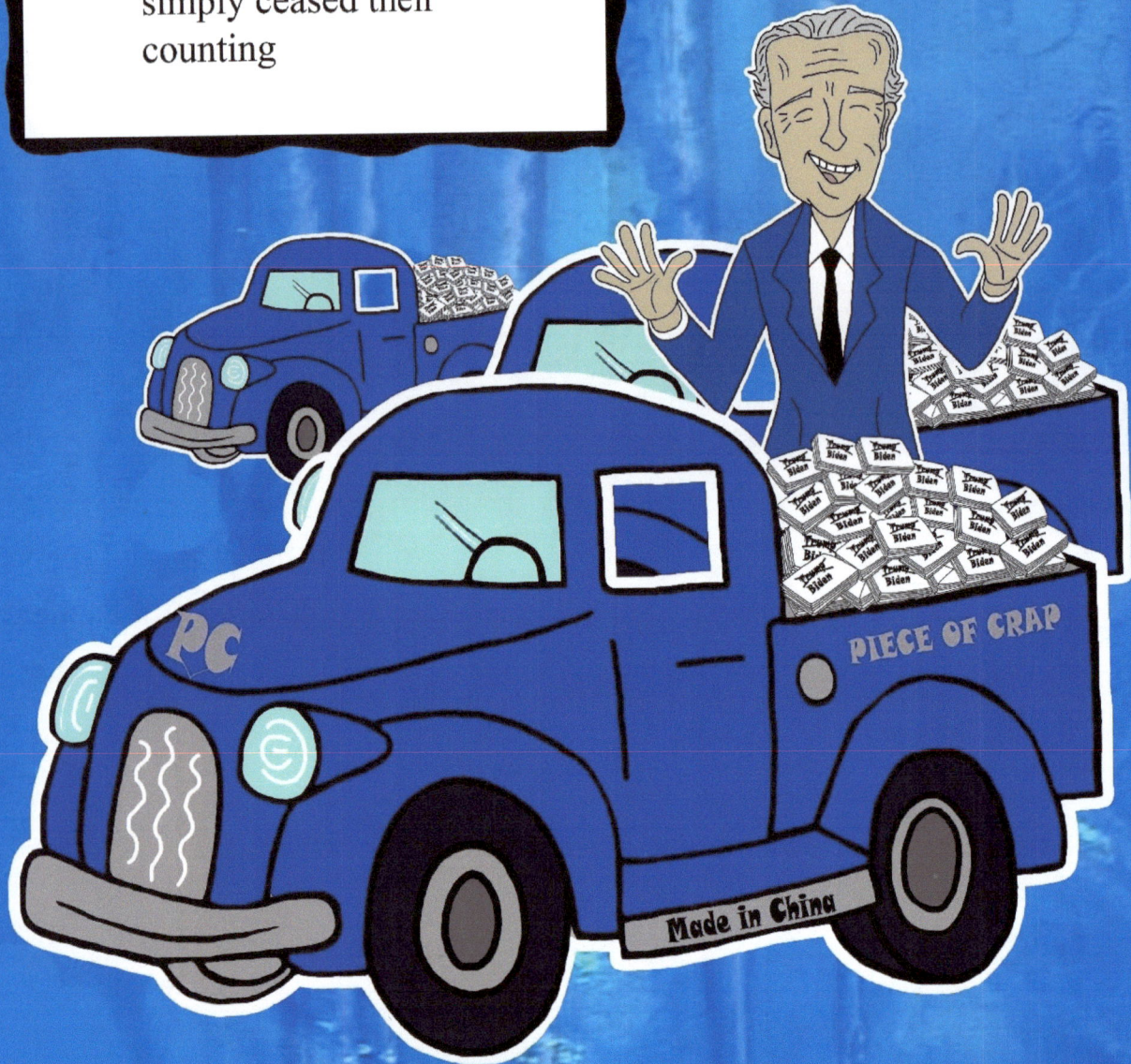

And if by miracle the next morning truckloads of ballots for Beijing Biden were mounting

Constitution-abiding, whistleblowers risked positions and reputations

James O'Keefe
@JamesOKeefeIII

Witnessing corruption? Contact Project Veritas.

We will tell your story.

VeritasTips@protonmail.com or on Signal 914-653-3110

10:42 AM · 3/25/21 · Twitter Web App

Fraud!

Dead people voted!

Voter Fraud!

[SOMALI] Waxaas waa absent ballots halkaas yaala soo uma jeedid fiiri waxaas oo dhan soo uma jeedidwaa buuxaa gaarigeyga.

All these here are absentee ballots. Can't you see? Look at all these, my car is full. My car is full.

Veritas **V.** The New York Times **NYT ANSWERS OUR COMPLAINT EXPOSENYT.COM**

Election Fraud!

Ballot Harvesting!

They appeared in videos with disguised voices and signed under-oath declarations

Fake news media clowns
lied to their viewers
As Americans
have grown to expect

Sorry!
AMERICA IS EXPERIENCING AN
ILLEGITIMATE
PRESIDENT
PLEASE STAND BY

JOE BIDEN ✓
ELECTED PRESIDENT
CNN PROJECTION
AKING NEWS
CNN PROJECTION
#CNNELECTION

Sorry!
AMERICA IS EXPERIENCING AN
ILLEGITIMATE
PRESIDENT
PLEASE STAND BY

They inaccurately and
prematurely announced
Sleepy China Joe Biden
President-select

Fortunately, smart Americans no longer fall for lamestream news and its deception

On January 2, 2013 Barack Obama signed and enacted into "law" HR 4310, also known as Smith-Mundt Modernization Act of 2012, which was part of the 2013 National Defense Authorization Act (NDAA). A large majority of concerned Americans were focused on the indefinite detention of US Citizens without trial clause contained in the NDAA, and missed HR 4310 which received little to no attention.

From Business Insider:

The NDAA Legalizes The Use Of Propaganda On The US Public

Smith-Mundt Modernization Act of 2012

BREAKING

Lamestream Media

Out Of Context Quotes

Non-existent Anonymous Sources

Fabricated Facts

Omitted Details

wearebreitbart

NYT: SWISS BILLIONAIRE BEHIND 'HUB PROJECT' TO INFLUENCE U.S. MEDIA, POLITICS; BIDS FOR TRIBUNE CO.

OCEANA

In 2013 Obama Legalized The Use Of Propaganda On The US Public

They're determined to expose the unconstitutionality of this very big, very rigged election

frankspeech.com

Powerful influential attorneys
have called it an international
criminal conspiracy

DOMINION VOTING

(Literally!)
CHANGING THE WAY PEOPLE VOTE

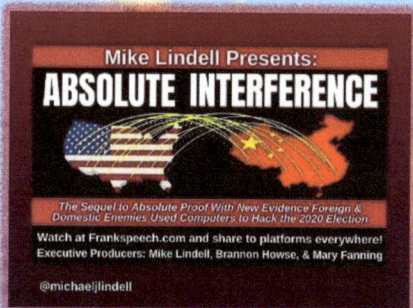

They say our elections
are run by foreign companies
the owners of which
are (temporarily) a mystery

Yes communists use computer and ballot fraud To interfere with our national elections

According to statistics from Newsweek, there are 600 organizations related to the CCP's "united front" in the United States, including at least 83 32 chambers of commerce, 10 "China Assistance Centers", media brands, and 38 organizations that promote "peaceful reunification," "Taiwan organizations, five educational and cultural organizations.

About half of the 70 Chinese professional associations in the United States are also related to the "united front." In addition, there are 265 Chinese Student and Scholar Associations in the United States. They often associate with the CCP's politics through the CCP's consulate educational affairs officials.

MARXISTS

COMMUNISTS

Statement by Donald J. Trump, 45th President of the United States of America

The New York Times did a story today saying that various Republican groups, many of them outstanding, are rallying on false claims that conservative activists are finding that the best way to raise money and keep voters engaged is to make Donald J. Trump's biggest fabrication, Election Fraud, their top priority. Sadly, the Election was Rigged, and without even going into detail, of which there is much, totally game changing. Democrats could not get Republican Legislatures in Swing States to approve many of the voting changes which took place before the Election, which is mandated under the Constitution of the United States. For that reason alone, we had an Illegitimate Election. The Supreme Court and other Courts were afraid to rule, they were "gutless," and will go down in history as such. No wonder so much money is being raised on this issue, and law-abiding people have every right to do so!

LIBERALS

U.S. media reveals that 600 CCP-related groups in the U.S. infiltrate, divide, and plot to subvert U.S. ambitions to surpass the election
October 27, 2020

DEMOCRATS

RADICAL LEFT

DOMESTIC TERRORISTS

WHY WOULD I ATTACK AMERICA?

YOU ALREADY HAVE DEMOCRATS FOR THAT.

But informed Americans will not accept the results of this very big, very rigged Presidential selection

Author C.G. Rousing, April 2020

Over 2 million members of the CCP

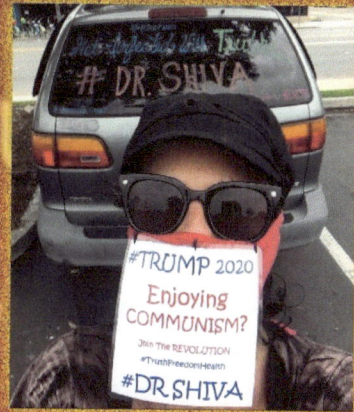

The Communist Manisfesto

by Karl Marx and Fredrich Engels

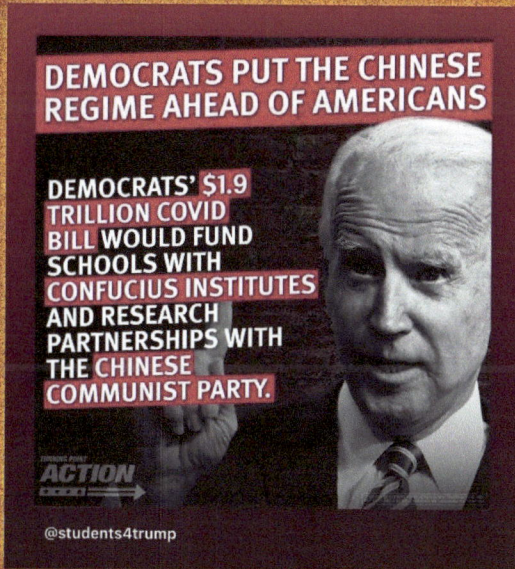

DEMOCRATS PUT THE CHINESE REGIME AHEAD OF AMERICANS

DEMOCRATS' $1.9 TRILLION COVID BILL WOULD FUND SCHOOLS WITH CONFUCIUS INSTITUTES AND RESEARCH PARTNERSHIPS WITH THE CHINESE COMMUNIST PARTY.

ACTION

@students4trump

According to statistics from Newsweek, there are 600 organizations related to the CCP's "united front" in the United States, including at least 83 fellow associations, 10 "China Assistance Centers", 32 chambers of commerce, 13 Chinese-language media brands, and 38 organizations that promote "peaceful reunification." "Taiwan organizations, five "friendship associations", and 129 other educational and cultural organizations.

About half of the 70 Chinese professional associations in the United States are also related to the "united front." In addition, there are 265 Chinese Student and Scholar Associations in the United States. They often associate with the CCP's politics through the CCP's consulate educational affairs officials.

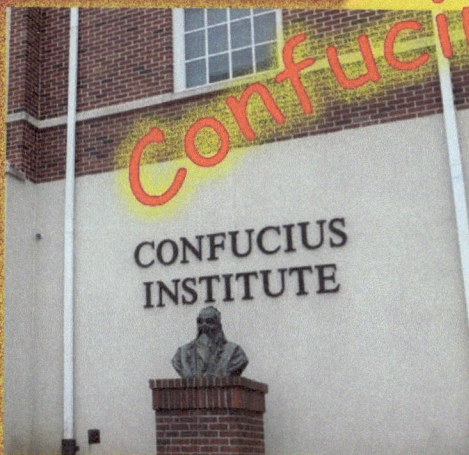

Confucius Institutes

CONFUCIUS INSTITUTE

Have been infiltrating America for decades – HOW CAN THAT BE?

They've bought high-ranking government officials, media outlets, celebrities, ivy league schools – too many to name

Judicial Watch PRESS RELEASE
BECAUSE NO ONE IS ABOVE THE LAW™

Judicial Watch Uncovers Documents Behind $1 Billion Mask Deal Between California and Chinese Communist Party Linked Company

CALIFORNIA REPUBLIC

DOMESTIC TERRORISTS

BILL GATES PRAISED COMMUNIST CHINA

wearebreitbart

WALL STREET, CORPORATIONS TEAM UP WITH SOROS-FUNDED GROUP TO PRESSURE STATES AGAINST ELECTION REFORMS

Sponsored By Parmesan Cheese

IF YOU REPEAT A LIE OFTEN ENOUGH...
Murdered by Ventilator
ACTION
IT BECOMES JOURNALISM

judicialwatch

FREE TRUMP
"FACEBOOK CENSORSHIP OF FORMER PRESIDENT TRUMP IS AN ATTACK ON THE FREE SPEECH OF EVERY AMERICAN. BIG TECH MUST STOP CENSORING CONSERVATIVES IN THEIR EFFORT TO HELP JOE BIDEN."
TOM FITTON, PRESIDENT, JUDICIAL WATCH

tomfitton • Following
TRUMP IS A CRIME **VICTIM!**
HUGE UPDATE

OBAMAGATE

THE DC PATRIOT
REAL NEWS IN REAL TIME

NEWS
Inventor Jovan Pulitzer Says He Was Offered $10M to Stay Quiet About Voter Fraud in 2020 Elections (VIDEO)

BENGHAZI

CONSTITUTION UNDER ATTACK
BY EXTREMIST LEFT

Like termites in the foundation of our freedom
They've pillaged our country and constitution for personal gain

The CCP released The China Virus And ignited World War III

One America News ✔ @OANN · 1h
President Trump: Dems won't be allowed to steal elections again, says Team Trump advancing effort to secure election integrity - oann.com/president-trum...
#OANN

students4trump

OUR HISTORIC, PATRIOTIC AND BEAUTIFUL MOVEMENT TO MAKE AMERICA GREAT AGAIN HAS ONLY JUST BEGUN. IN THE MONTHS AHEAD I HAVE MUCH TO SHARE WITH YOU...

PRESIDENT DONALD J. TRUMP

TURNING POINT
ACTION

BIDEN IS A TOTALITARIAN COMMUNIST.
DAN BONGINO

But the historical movement initiated by Donald J. Trump will ensure that America remains FREE

Fortunately for Americans
and really people everywhere

Who FACT CHECKS the FACT-CHECKERS?

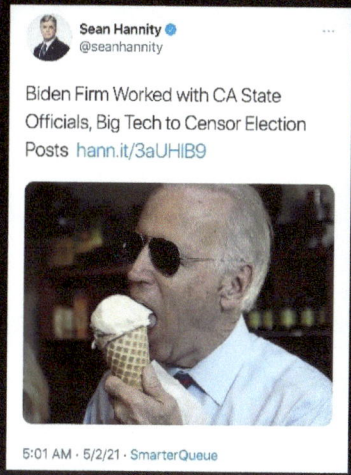

▶ PROJECT VERITAS

Charlie Chester, CNN Technical Director

We were, we were creating a story there that we
didn't know anything about, you know?

#ExposeCNN VISIT PROJECTVERITAS.COM/BRAVE

CNN EXPOSED: STAFFER ADMITS THAT NETWORK'S
FOCUS "WAS TO GET TRUMP OUT OF OFFICE"

BREAKING NEWS

HEIR CONDITIONS OVER ATTACKS ON AFGHANS... OFFICIALS ALSO SAY ALL 2,500 U.S. TROOPS WILL BE

FOX NEWS channel

FrankSpeech.com

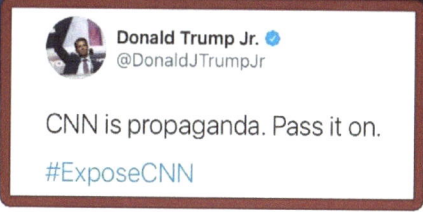

Patriots are exposing fake news
And helping others become aware

That propagandists
Disguised as journalists
Lie to We The People every day

TREASON

That mainstream media is a hoax
And freedom is the price we pay

Fake news outlets
are willing participants
in this illicit ruse

Candace Owens ✓
@RealCandaceO

Fake Election
Fake Inauguration
Fake Press Conference

America is looking more and more like a
communist country.

9:06 PM · 3/25/21 · Twitter for iPhone

15.6K Retweets 608 Quote Tweets 77.4K Likes

FAKE NEWS

► PROJECT VERITAS ey

JAMES O'KEEFE
FOUNDER & CEO, PROJECT VERITAS

You're on camera talking about the
importance of, "...getting Trump out of office..."

#ExposeCNN VISIT PROJECTVERITAS.COM/BRAVE

FOX NEWS
6:40 PT

PROJECT VERITAS CONFRONTS CNN STAFFER
WHO ADMITTED HIS NETWORK SPEWS PROPAGANDA

BREAKING NEWS

PROPAGANDA

NYT Journalist Erases ENTIRE Twitter
After National Pulse Unearths Posts
Admitting 'Working' For The Chinese
Communist Party.

@maganewsnetwork

Spewing propaganda
and lies to the public
is journalistic abuse

project_veritas   •••

CNN's technical director
Charlie Chester
Confessed on tape
For the entire world to see

NO SHOW

Project Veritas

Charlie Chester, CNN Technical Director

Our (CNN) focus was to get Trump out of office, right?
Without saying it, that's what it was. Right?

#ExposeCNN VISIT PROJECTVERITAS.COM/BRAVE

CNN EXPOSED

That CNN's focus was to
"Get Trump Out Of Office"
and to LIE to you and me

CENTRAL CITY

Investigative Report
How the Election Was Stolen

The election was stolen
The election was rigged

...he Century

How Election Was Stolen

Analysis Shows Obvious Fraud By Computer in States of GA, PA

Woody Jenkins
Editor

CENTRAL — Election Day in the United States, held this year on Tuesday, Nov. 3, 2020, was really a series of 51 separate elections — one in each of the 50 states and the District of Columbia. The vote total in each determines how the electoral votes of that state or district will be cast in the Electoral College on Dec. 14, 2020.

Thirty of those states and more than 2,600 counties have something in common. The citizens of those areas vote on voting machines provided by Dominion Voting Systems with software from Smartmatic Vote Counting System.

While supporters of President Trump cast about for evidence of vote fraud in the form of unsigned ballots, mishandled paper ballots, and evidence of "retail" vote fraud,

President Donald Trump

Former Vice President Joe Biden

Fake Votes Were Reported in Multiples of 4,800 Votes in GA, 6,000 in PA in Identical Fashion

proof of massive computer-based vote fraud is right before the nation's eyes. It is going unnoticed in this hyper-partisan atmosphere.

Ironically, The New York Times, a vocal critic of the President, has recorded the fraud for all times, even though they have not reported it.

While the mainstream media has crowned former Vice President Joe Biden as "President-elect," the facts on the ground are quite different, at least in two swing states that have been called for Vice President Biden — Georgia and Pennsylvania.

In those two states, a careful analysis of the data shows that both states voted for President Trump and the election was stolen.

It was fraud by computer.

Since Dominion and Smartmatic have control of the voting machines, the software, and the reporting of the results, it should be up to the owners and officials of those two entities to explain how it was done. But it was done, as will be shown.

Unraveling this mystery begins with The New York Times. After polls closed on Election Day, The Times began to report the results hour after hour. The coding for that data is still online, and we have downloaded it in case it is taken down.

The data from The Times shows the time, expressed as UTC, or Universal time, which is Greenwich mean time in England.

It also shows the totals for Trump and Biden, Trump's lead, and then new votes for Trump and Biden as each change in the results was uploaded. Then it shows something very significant. The increase or de

See GEORGIA on Page 6

New York Times Election Report Reveals
104,984 Stolen Vot...

Millions of Mail Ballots Made It Impossible to Track Which Votes Were Being Tabulated

Woody Jenkins
Editor

CENTRAL — After every election, the Central City News publishes precinct-by-precinct voting returns

The repercussions are many
The consequences BIG

2020 Presidential

Timestamp	UTC	Tr...						
11/4/2020	16:35	2.38...						0
11/4/2020	17:12	2.38...						4
11/4/2020	19:42	2.39...						1
11/4/2020	20:12	2.3...						1
11/4/2020	21:43	2.40...						2
11/4/2020	22:52	2.41...						2
11/5/2020	0:18	2,420,607	2,372,097	48,510	3,494	12,995	-9,501	2
11/5/2020	1:26	2,428,156	2,389,149	39,007	2,365	11,971	-9,606	2

19

Donald J. Trump was elected
In an absolute nationwide
landslide

Donald J. Trump ✓ @realDonald... ·3h ···
This Election was RIGGED, but we will
WIN!

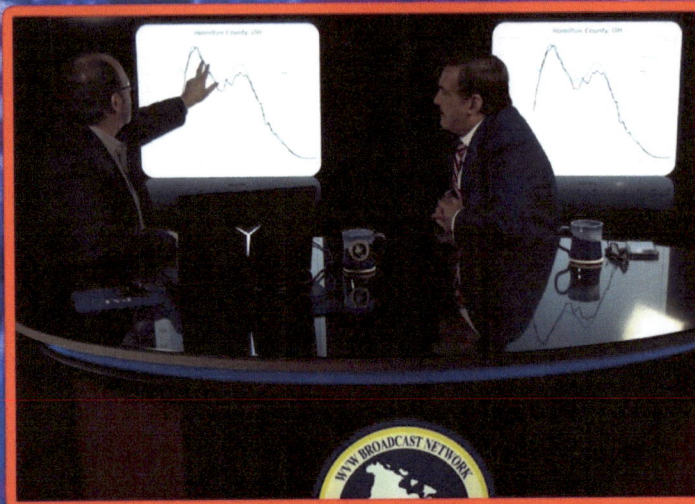

Mike Lindell Presents:
ABSOLUTE INTERFERENCE
The Sequel to Absolute Proof With New Evidence Foreign &
Domestic Enemies Used Computers to Hack the 2020 Election
Watch at Frankspeech.com and share to platforms everywhere!
Executive Producers: Mike Lindell, Brannon Howse, & Mary Fanning
@michaeljlindell

The voice of WE THE PEOPLE
was silenced
Our actual votes cast aside

But truth
Has a way of prevailing
In the land of the free
And the brave

To tyranny and corruption and
those who attempt to impose it
Patriots shall never cave

If ever in doubt just remember
The best protection against a
government gone rogue

Is a copy of the constitution
Your favorite gun
And your Made-in-the-USA robe

THE BEGINNING

IMAGINE IF YOU WILL

A WORLD WHERE MEMES ARE FACT CHECKED BUT BALLOTS AREN'T...

maganewsnetwork

USA TODAY

Is Donald Trump still president? On Republican websites across Florida, the answer is yes

Joshua Solomon, Treasure Coast Newspapers
Fri, March 19, 2021, 1:30 PM · 3 min read

Donald Trump

At least 10 local Republican Party websites across Florida continue to show Donald Trump as the current president of the United States, more than four months after he lost the election to Joe Biden.

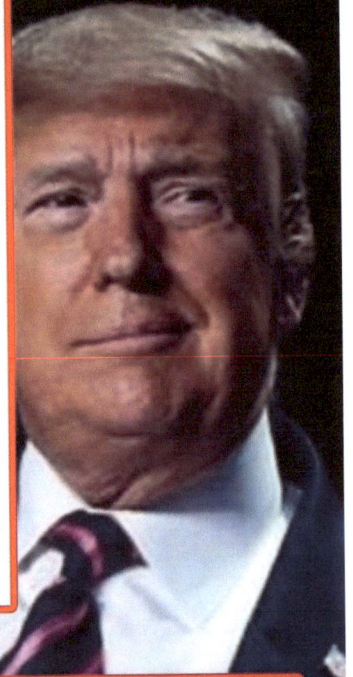

Jenna Ellis
@JennaEllisEsq

45 >>>>> 46*

*rigged

10:24 PM · 4/28/21 · Twitter for iPhone

77% OF AMERICANS
APPROVE OF REQUIRING PHOTO ID TO VOTE

@sentedcruz

ABOUT THE AUTHOR

C.G. Rousing is a San Diego-based, American author, illustrator, publishing consultant, mother, songwriter, pianist, medium, truth-seeker, and founder of Paranormal-Con.

To learn more about Rousing and to order signed copies of

THE VERY BIG VERY RIGGED 2020 PRESIDENTIAL ELECTION

Along with her other books:

LAW AND ORDER: A Tribute To #45

THOUGHTS TO DIE FOR

THE INTENDERS: WE MUST TELL THE PEOPLE

Visit:

CGRousing.com

www.ingramcontent.com/pod-product-compliance
Lightning Source LLC
Chambersburg PA
CBHW040022050426
42452CB00002B/90